T0295603

Ideas of Europe

Ideas of Europe is a critical essay reassessing the founding myths of Europe and the making of a European identity from antiquity to the present age. Antonelli argues that the intrinsic fragility and precarious nature of the perceived geographical entity of Europe has been compensated by the creation of a strong and wide European cultural identity, which has embraced Latin tradition as interpreted and appropriated by Germanic, Romance, Slavonic, as well as Greek and Byzantine cultures to form the European cultural space as we know it today. The development of a creative relationship between antiquity and modernity, and the birth of a European Literature have created a 'time' of and for Europe. The method used throughout the book is rigorously historical-philological on the one hand, while on the other it is enriched through critical dialogue with the great authors of the European tradition − from the classical Greek-Latin figures to the literati and philosophers of the nineteenth and twentieth centuries. This critical history of the cultural representations of Europe is a vital text for readers from across the humanities and social sciences who are interested in cultural history and in the values of Europe.

Roberto Antonelli is the current President of the Accademia Nazionale dei Lincei. Emeritus Professor of Romance Philology at Rome "La Sapienza", he has been Membre étranger de l'Académie des Inscriptions et Belles Lettres since 2016. He was President of the Société de Linguistique Romane (2016– 2019), President of the *Ateneo federato delle Scienze umane, delle Arti e dell'Ambiente* at Rome "La Sapienza" (2008–2010) and Dean of the Faculty of Humanities (2004–2008) at Rome "La Sapienza". He has published widely on all fields of Romance Studies, from the Middle Ages to the present day. He has promoted major EU research projects on the *European Literary Canon* and the *Lexicon of Emotions in European Literature*.

Ideas of Europe
Time, Space, and Tradition

Roberto Antonelli

Translated from the Italian by Nadia Cannata, revised by
Margaret J-M. Sönmez

Routledge
Taylor & Francis Group

LONDON AND NEW YORK

First published 2024
by Routledge
4 Park Square, Milton Park, Abingdon, Oxon OX14 4RN

and by Routledge
605 Third Avenue, New York, NY 10158

Routledge is an imprint of the Taylor & Francis Group, an informa business

© 2024 Roberto Antonelli

British Library Cataloguing-in-Publication Data
A catalogue record for this book is available from the British Library

Library of Congress Cataloging-in-Publication Data
Names: Antonelli, Roberto, author. | Cannata Salomone, Nadia, translator.
Title: Ideas of Europe: time, space, and tradition / Roberto Antonelli, Nadia Cannata.
Other titles: Magazzini della memoria. English
Description: First. | New York : Routledge, 2024. | Full original title: I Magazzini della Memoria : Luoghi i Tempi dell'Europa | Includes bibliographical references and index. |
Identifiers: LCCN 2023038489 (print) | LCCN 2023038490 (ebook) | ISBN 9781032425801 (hardback) | ISBN 9781032425818 (paperback) | ISBN 9781003363323 (ebook)
Subjects: LCSH: Europe--History--Philosophy. | Europe--Civilization. | Europeans--Ethnic identity.
Classification: LCC D16.8 .A6399 2024 (print) | LCC D16.8 (ebook) | DDC 305.809--dc23/eng/20230914
LC record available at https://lccn.loc.gov/2023038489
LC ebook record available at https://lccn.loc.gov/2023038490

ISBN: 9781032425801 (hbk)
ISBN: 9781032425818 (pbk)
ISBN: 9781003363323 (ebk)

DOI: 10.4324/9781003363323

Typeset in Times New Roman
by Deanta Global Publishing Services, Chennai, India

Contents

1 Europe's space

Land and sea

From the sky, the geographical space called Europe (whose name comes from the Semitic *ereb*, "west") appears today, as it did for Paul Valery, as a rather non-descript western Asian peninsula, a vast hinterland faintly outlined by the Urals to the East. In the well-known myth, Jove, taking the semblance of a bull, kidnapped Europe and left the land to cross the Hellespont, pointing westwards towards Crete, where Europe gave birth to Minos, the king philosopher, educated by Jove himself. According to Dante, Minos was a lawmaker as well as the keeper of the doors of Hell. He was also the husband of Pasifae, mother of the Minotaur and in some way the initiator of the history of Greece – since its beginnings are conventionally identified with the Minotaur's defeat by Theseus. The power of Athens and its dominion over the earth and the seas made of the Hellespont a bridge connecting two continents.

It has been argued that all the founding myths and in all the symbols of Europe feature the concept of a dual space – land and sea – born from a single root[1]: Asia and its lands precipitated into the seas as Europe, a peninsula full of harbours, as well as islands. In the first occurrences of the denomination *Europe*, to be found in Herodotus and later Isocrates,[2] the name incarnates the geographical and cultural space of the Greeks and covers both the Greek peninsula and its islands, as well as Thracia and, later, the western colonies of Greece.

Europe bears a dual identity, characterized by conflict and change: Jove mutated into a bull, in order to kidnap Europe; the Minotaur, fruit of his encounter with Europe, is half man and half beast (as indeed every man somehow is). In Aeschylus' *Persians*, Xerxe's mother sees her son being ejected from his chariot as he was striving to subjugate two women "of perfect beauty" under one yoke:

> one sister carried her restraint with pride
> and kept her mouth compliant in the reins

(192–194)

DOI: 10.4324/9781003363323-1

While this one, Asia, appeared tame, the other was unruly and it was she who was responsible for Perseus' fall. She was Greek, and her restlessness was induced by her recognition – as Europe – of her otherness with respect to the vast plains of the Asian continent. Sisters in blood, they inhabited different spaces, the one stretching towards the sea and the islands, the other "subjugated" to earth and inhabiting a "foreign land" (190–198).

Europe is provided with a double identity, and hence she is unruly: in *Persians* the conflict she embodies is presented as the contrast between political freedom and Asian tyrannies:

> the city of Athens remains unscathed.
> Yes. While its citizens are still alive,
> it has a fortress that will never fail.
>
> (395–397)

Freedom allows for an orderly fleet which is contrasted to the disorder in the Persian and Barbarian lines. The sea for the Asians is "an immense sea of evil" (435), while Spartans are the most valiant because, in Herodotus' words, they are "free, yet not wholly free" (*Histories*, VII, 104). Nomos, the Law, rules over them and they fear it more than the Persians fear Xerxes. They will always obey its invariable command, which is never to retreat from the enemy, always to hold your position and either to win or to die. Greeks fight in their own interest, and do not ever live in servitude (*ibid*). Consequently, they are the best fighters.

Aristotle (*Politics*, VII, 1327b) characterizes the Greeks through their ability to change, face conflict, and stand up to all enemies, as well as through their will to replace tyranny and the eastern Persian Empire. Placed in an intermediate position between peoples from colder lands (full of courage, but lacking in intelligence and knowledge) and Asian peoples (provided with intelligence and knowledge, but lacking in courage) the Greeks are courageous and intelligent, and therefore they live in freedom, enjoy the best political organizations and could dominate over all peoples if only they were part of a single political system (which they would be in Aristotle's lifetime).

However, all this would not have been physically identifiable in a geographical space had the Greeks not discovered the sea and, through their relations with it, established their identity as free people capable of organizing fleets and negotiating routes, thus effecting democracy and establishing commercial relations.

When Hegel attempted to define the European spirit across the centuries he, too, would refer to the sea, and claimed that,

> For Asia the sea has no significance. On the contrary, the Asian peoples have shut themselves off from the sea [...] In India, religion positively prohibits going out to sea. The Egyptians, too, at the time of their greatest

flourishing, had no navigation on the sea, although river navigation was very lively. Thus seafaring is excluded from the Asian principle, while in Europe it plays a large role.

(204)

The European State is truly European only in so far as it has links with the sea. The sea provides that wholly peculiar outlet which Asiatic life lacks.

Europe's shifting space

In its history and character Europe's space seems to reflect the mythical and archetypical origins which define it in contrast with Asia. Europe is, as it were, *in motion* since its very beginnings; it is a shifting space, subject to expansion and contraction, and constantly in search of a definition. From Greece and Thracia going westwards towards the Adriatic Sea, Sicily and the Spanish shores, the spirit of Greece transferred to Rome and sat at the foundations of the Romance world.

However, the original idea of Europe could not sustain its enormous expansion: freedom and political power were based on the plurality of city states, which united occasionally against external enemies, and eventually were directed by Alexander the Great to conquer the East. The encounter of West and East created an empire whose oriental part was significantly greater than its Greek origins and whose civilisation would be Hellenistic, not Hellenic and European (western and centrally placed between north, south, and east).

When Rome was to unify the Mediterranean something similar would occur. The *urbs*, a western city-state would become *Orbis*, i.e. the world (and it was even suggested the two had a common etymology). The idea of Europe would thus be lost – even though the conception that Greece was somehow transferred to Rome established a narrative which would define the future of European culture and civilization. As Horace put it, "*Graecia capta ferum victorem cepit*," Captive Greece captured, in turn, her uncivilized conquerors (2.1, l. 156). At the time the Mediterranean was at the centre of the world (literally in the middle of the known lands), between west and east, linguistically and culturally divided between Latin and Greek, and eventually also by religion and politics.

The Roman Empire would remain the only dominion known to history to comprise under one rule all the lands we now call the Mediterranean, and the only instance of a political body embracing the cultures and peoples of all the three continents known at the time. Up to the present, even after the Arab conquests, the Mediterranean has maintained a mythical aura and a geopolitical and cultural uniqueness. Defined by the multifarious presence of innumerable races and cultures, and by their encounters, overlaps, and confrontation, it has maintained its distinct otherness within the newly formed western idea of Europe.

Perceived as both East and South, the Mediterranean is an integral part of the history and identity of Europe, yet it is also perceived as problematic by north-European modernity. It sums up the idea of otherness on various levels (cultural, existential, spatial), and is unified by rites, customs, and languages all linked somehow to the archetypical origins of Europe. As claimed by Matvejevic (12), "internal links resists all divisions. The Mediterranean is not merely belonging." This also applies to Eastern Europe, *mutatis mutandis*, where the founding archetypes take us to Constantinople-Byzantium.

The Mediterranean Sea is therefore both a real and a symbolic space. A liminal space travelled by the Greeks westwards and by the Romans eastwards until a further journey operated the ultimate *translatio* from east to west – that of Jesus Christ and Saint Paul. Christian thought, historiography, and writings, including those of Dante, would justify the Empire as functional in providing a setting for the birth of Jesus in a world both unified and pacified. Such a world was thus ready to welcome the Christian message, which permanently altered the conception of time and space, and produced a synthesis of the Old with a New Testament. Such a message was addressed to the whole *Orbis*, to Rome and beyond, to the north, and to the cold lands inhabited by the Barbarians which, until then, had been excluded from classical civilization. Thus, both internal (slaves) and external lower orders (Barbarians) became protagonists of history and of cultural and religious life.

However, when migrations of Barbarians caused the division into Western and Eastern Empires, the term *Roman* would be reserved for the subjects of the (Greek) Eastern Empire, whereas in the West it would be kept symbolically to mark the continuity with the great empire of antiquity. The concept of a Sacred, or Holy Roman Empire would embrace the passage from East to West of culture, religion, and language – Greek to Latin – and the movement from Athens to Rome and eventually to Aachen, but it would define a thoroughly new entity in terms of both time and space.

Christian Europe

Charlemagne, the first Emperor of the new Christian dominion, got the titles of *Rex pater Europae, patricius Romanorum*, and *dominus Europae*, no doubt in reference to the geographical extension of his lands. *Pater Europae*, contrary to what has been argued by Chabod,[3] implies more than just a physical space; it stretches to culture and anthropology. But Charlemagne was considered father to what idea of Europe? Once the Western Empire had collapsed, only the Eastern Empire of Byzantium survived, its prestige ensured by its perceived continuity with the ancient Empire, although in language and religion it differed profoundly from the west.

The continuity of the Imperial power, and the Greek nature of its culture and religion (further confirmed by the Great Schism of 1054), would survive to effect borders still visible today and underlie tragedies to come. But Europe would never again extend from the Atlantic to the Urals (that faint outline to the East), it would stop way before them.

Religious differences were strengthened by ancestral fears of the vast and unknown eastern lands, open to foreign people entering the civil space from lands not marked by walls and cities (Barbarians carried their homes on wagons).

Gibraltar (the pillars of Hercules) to the West marks a boundary beyond which only the legendary Fortunate Isles or the Isles of the Blessed were known, inhabited by demigods and heroes of classical literature and mythology: the known seas are the Mediterranean or the Pontus, seas which are surrounded by known lands. The Ocean is so 'other' that it marks an end, not a beginning; it may feel darker than the Eastern plains, but it is "a world that is unpeopled" (Dante, *Inf.* XXVI.117), the seat of the afterlife, not of this life. Despite the Carthaginians having circumnavigated Africa and the Atlantic islands, the Ocean never became a known part of the ancient world or indeed of medieval space. It lived as a fantastic world, not necessarily dark, despite being associated with the sunset. No threat came from the West: people simply never came back from it.

On the other hand, news from terrifying and unknown peoples from Asia, as well as of myths and fantasies to haunt dreams, would reach the Mediterranean and the Roman world. The idea of the dark powers of the Scythians and of the peoples from the steppes, evoked by the migrations (or invasions, depending on the point of view) of the so-called Barbarians would constitute – as in many discourses they do to this day – an obscure and threatening idea of otherness with respect to the western *respublica christiana*. Once the Eastern Empire collapsed and continuity with the ancient Roman civilization was all but lost, only the apparently restless movements of fiery and dangerous peoples roaming plains without cities or walls would, it seemed, remain. By the end of the fifteenth century, Eastern Christianity migrated to the third Rome, i.e. Moscow, thus establishing the ultimate bastion against the nomads from the steppes and the seeming infinity of Asia. In a way, Europe extended again to the Urals, but in so doing it had to become in part Asian, non-European, an Empire across both East and West.

Only after 1917 and then 1945 – and for conflicting reasons also after 1989 – would the question of how to integrate the two Europes become a burning issue. A form of deletion of memory, accepted in the current narrative, has contrasted the history of Eastern Europe with that of the Latin West, from as early as the reign of Charlemagne.[4] Even Dante, in his treaty on language, excluded Scythians and Slavs from the three families of European languages (Romance, Germanic, and Greek)[5] and noted that Scythians lived "beyond the seventh zone and are exposed to nights and days of very unequal length, and endure an almost unbearable intensity of cold" (*Monarchia* I. xiv, 6).

Charlemagne was *dominus*, *rex* and *pater* of a Europe comprising France, a small portion of Spain, a significant part of Germany (extending well beyond the boundaries of the *limes romanus* [Roman border defence] and roughly half of Italy, including Rome). Europe no longer embraced the Mediterranean, for that region was cut in two and largely dominated by the Arabs. The Holy Roman Empire constituted Charlemagne's Europe, which moved its centre northwards, along the Rome-Aachen axis, and which connected Church and Empire. The European space thus acquired more or less the shape of the first nucleus of the European Community, as it was established in 1957 by the Treaty of Rome. The religious confrontation became also political as soon as the alliance between the Pope and the Emperor produced a new Empire, Holy and Roman, which would consolidate its territories as it sought to establish its own legitimacy. The idea of Europe embraced a geographic territory as well as a culture markedly distancing itself from antiquity and the Latin tradition, even though it had largely issued from it.

The migrations of the groups that Romans and Greeks had called Barbarians brought to the fore differences between peoples and regions not unbeknown to the Romans: as the people slowly broke away from Roman space (and time) a new geographical space was created, and new languages were established, as were new cultural identities which became part of the new European Empire established by Charlemagne. The new Europe was not exclusively characterized as Barbaric or Nordic (even though to a large extent it looked northwards), and it embraced those parts of Italy which did not remain Byzantine but had fallen to the Longobards.

The peoples of the older empire had embraced within their boundaries citizens of all nations, speaking a vast variety of languages. In accordance with the new Christian message, which stretched beyond the *urbs* and the heavenly city, they welcomed immigrants irrespective of their different habits, laws, and secular institutions, as noted by Augustine (*De Civitate Dei* [*City of God*] XIX, 17). Populations originating outside of the Roman world, or at its margins, chose (or were forced to choose) a religion and culture profoundly different, and technically superior, to their own, and made a formidable effort of cultural elevation, which would represent the most significant novelty to mark the future of the western and Christian Europe as opposed to its eastern counterpart.

At the time of Charlemagne these different languages and peoples acquired an institutional representation, and in such institutions, as even Augustine had recognized, we spend our lives (*De Doctrina Christiana*, II xl, 60). Europe therefore became also the seat of the Roman church: according to Chabod (30), the Romans, as opposed to the Greeks in Byzantium, constituted the *regnum ecclesiae*, a dominion of the Church. Europe came to coincide with Western Christianity, politically subjected to Charlemagne's Empire, whilst Eastern Christianity belonged to the Emperor in Constantinople.

If Western Christianity constitutes a unity, and Europe is a direct issue from the Western Roman Empire, the terms *Christian* and *European* reflect the same identity and thus justified (from its perspective) Europe's expansion towards all other peoples, as it justified most of all the effort to get back the lands associated with the very origin of Christianity, namely the crusades in the East and the *reconquista* of Spain in the West. The word *Europeans* was used in the eighth century by Isidorus Paciensis (Isidore of Beja) to describe the crucial battle in Poitiers through which Charles Martel stopped the advance of the Arabs in Europe in 732, and Isidore's use of the term marks both a geographic and an ideological boundary: he wrote *prospiciunt Europeenses Arabum tentoria ordinata* (Migne 8271), "the Europeans see in front of them the orderly tents of the Arabs."

Using Christian and moral terms, the Crusades can be said to have revisited the legitimacy of domination by Greece and Rome. Through force and the Gospel, the geo-political space of Western Europe would slowly spread to embrace all Latin and Germanic peoples and unite them in a *respublica christiana* represented by the Roman Church. Within this Western European space, some Slavonic peoples remained isolated because of not sharing the Latin alphabet or language, which dominated both religion and cultural transmission.

It could be argued, therefore, that Europe as an idea is a complex metaphor, whose vehicle was comprised by the Latin language, the Bible (the book *par excellence*), and the network of texts and relations which were written and conducted in Latin wherever (western) Christianity reached. Throughout the ten centuries which count as the Western Middle Ages (a period which stretched longer than the Roman domination of Europe) unity was represented by the Latin language. The Western Roman Empire did not exist anymore, but its language endured, and guaranteed unity and tradition through the only possible form of Christian Empire, the foundation constituted by God's book translated into Latin; both language and book stood at the root of Medieval Europe and of Western culture.

Identity and otherness

Through the *long durée* of the Middle Ages Latin constituted the most significant and persistent cultural institution preserved and nurtured in the ideal space constructed between Rome and Aachen. It ensured the continuity of Europe's tradition and the memory of its history. For centuries, literature, jurisprudence, and science were written in Latin, and university textbooks in some various subjects were still being written in Latin as late as the nineteenth century. Assuming that a language does constitute an intellectual paradigm and, to an extent, a structure for thought, then it may be argued that a European underlying and all-embracing grammar does exist and is identifiable with Latin.

Medieval Latin, however subject to variation, was essentially unitary – one – just as the Empire was one and the Church was one. The collapse of the Roman Empire did, however, make internal differences more conspicuous and more significant: Charlemagne tried to rebuild a linguistic canon for the ruling classes of the new empire, whilst acknowledging that Latin was no longer understood by the people and that contact with his subjects and the way they worshipped was thereby weakened. In 813 the Council of Tours ruled that sermons during mass should be delivered in rustic Roman or in the German language, so that "everyone could better understand what is being said."[6] One single international language slowly gave way to many different ones, through a process that started within the Roman Empire and was accelerated by the invasions. It would take more than a further 1000 years for the use of local languages to be allowed in the liturgy, and for the official Vatican newspaper to stop being printed in Latin.

It is not without significance that this all happened in Charlemagne's Empire and age. Europe's cultural space took different shapes according to what it embraced – literature, philosophy, institutions, or architecture. Each of the arts designed its own geographical spaces, relations between people and with the international organizations which supported or exercised them: the Roman church, as well as monasteries, universities, new ecclesiastical orders, whose libraries ensured that a canon of authors, unified by the common language, had a known seat, and could be kept and transmitted widely.

The written tradition of the new languages followed similar patterns across the Romance and the Germanic worlds, but with timings dependent upon the individual and specific socio-political and cultural contexts. The result was however the same: the creation of new traditions somewhat independent of Latin and of Church and Empire, the two overpowering international institutions. The first texts to be written in the new languages were legal and religious documents, later came texts of a literary nature, intended for a different public, and different occasions. Latin was still used for high office and wherever prestige was needed, or when there was an intention to direct the message to a wider, international audience or to the scholarly community. Local vernaculars were common in written productions of a practical nature, or when the intention was to reach a general public interested in new genres (lyric poetry, romance), linked mostly to love. Such literary genres are unique features of medieval European literature, unknown to preceding traditions. The new languages of Europe were used according to the style required by the narration, the function they had in the text, or as part of characterization.

The literary genres and different languages and styles evolved according to the public and context for which they were intended: court, piazza, university. In the sixteenth century Dante was accused by a university professor, Giovanni del Virgilio, of casting his pearls before swine, since he wrote his *Comedia* in the vernacular rather than in Latin. The destiny of Latin was nonetheless evident in the late Middle Ages, despite its continuing importance and endurance:

the language of modern European literatures would be made up of some of the developing vernaculars gradually extended to function as national languages.

Between the nineteenth and twentieth centuries the languages and peoples of modern Europe had acquired more or less the outlines they have today. It could be argued that the history of the written languages in European territories represents, symbolically, the history of Europe: from unity to diversity. When Luther translated the Bible into German his book and its language formed the basis of a newly recognized identity, national as well as religious, and social. The Reformation divided Christian Europe internally along lines which had to do with religion, anthropology, economy and culture, and which separated, roughly speaking, Romance Europe from the Germanic peoples. England, despite some acquired roots in Romance culture, was linguistically divided. Further, especially England's insularity and position towards the Atlantic enabled it to acquire a hegemonic position with respect to the other European nations when large parts of America were explored and conquered in the fifteenth century and Europe projected itself overseas. Within the Catholic world, the possibility of the laity reading the Bible in their own languages challenged the power of the Roman church and prompted it to reassess the centrality of the book, but along lines which led from the original unity of the *respublica christiana* to a plurality of interpretations reflected in geography and culture.

Diversity and power

In 842, in Strasbourg, Charles the Bald and Ludwig the German, grandchildren of Charlemagne, chose to swear their alliance against Lotharius not in Latin, but each in the language that the other's army would understand. The Oath of Strasbourg thus constituted the first written, official recognition of the French and German vernaculars, and was a landmark in European history, marking the weakening of the central Imperial power and the growing influence of rising national entities. This development, with growing local authorities and a progressively more distant centre, favoured a dialectic between unity and diversity which would soon result in the drawing up of the *Magna Carta Libertatum* and the establishment in England of the first parliament in Europe, whilst in Italy and Germany city states and regional states flourished, as a consequence of the weakening of the central imperial rule and of clashes between these two major international powers.

The power of a king in Europe would never be tyrannical and absolute as in Asia, as had been heralded in more ancient times when the unruly and freedom-liking Greek politics came into conflict with the Asian model of tyranny, probably the first occurrence of an awareness of a Greek, and European, founding identity. As Machiavelli famously wrote in *The Prince*:

> the principalities of which one has record are found to be governed in two different ways; either by a prince, with a body of servants, who assist him

to govern the kingdom as ministers by his favour and permission; or by a prince and barons, who hold that dignity by antiquity of blood and not by the grace of the prince. Such barons have states and their own subjects, who recognize them as lords and hold them in natural affection. Those states that are governed by a prince and his servants hold their prince in more consideration, because in all the country there is no one who is recognized as superior to him, and if they yield obedience to another they do it as to a minister and official, and they do not bear him any particular affection.

The examples of these two governments in our time are the Turk and the King of France. The entire monarchy of the Turk is governed by one lord, the others are his servants […]. But the King of France is placed in the midst of an ancient body of lords, acknowledged by their own subjects, and beloved by them; they have their own prerogatives, nor can the king take these away except at his peril.

(Chapter 4)

Machiavelli claimed in his *Art of War* that Europe's internal diversity was the reason for its military success:

You know of the men excellent in war there have been many famed in Europe, few in Africa, and less in Asia. This results from (the fact that) these last two parts of the world have had a Principality or two, and few Republics; but Europe alone has had some Kingdoms and an infinite number of Republics. […]. The world has been more virtuous when there have been many States which have favored virtue, either from necessity or from other human passion.

(Book II)

And in his *Discourses on the First Decade of Livy* he further argued that internal discord, or plurality of points of view, can be a progressive and positive attribute, for if potential conflicts are dealt with within the state the result may be a virtuous circle and an enhancement of power:

for good examples proceed from good education and a good education from good laws, and good laws from those tumults which many unadvisedly do condemn: for whosoever shall examine the end thereof, shall not find that they produced any banishment or violence in hinderance of the common good, but laws and ordinances in benefit of the public liberty.

(I, 4)

Embracing an identity which stems from plurality would be a defining feature of European intellectual awareness, as (Western) Europe is a complex system made of multiple identities, inevitably exposed to some conflict, but nonetheless characterized by a common bond.

In Chapter 197 of *Essais sur les Moeurs*, Voltaire elaborated and further developed the idea of a political and cultural European common identity that he took from Montesquieu, who argued in his *Lettres Persanes* that Europe formed a plural system as opposed to the Asian power that was still defined by despotism and inability to change.[7]

Voltaire underlines the traits of a Christian European unity, which may evoke Carolingian overtones were it not for its geographic expansion with respect to the Holy Roman Empire and the multiplicity of states and political identities it housed.

> For a long time past, the Christian part of Europe—Russia excepted—might be considered as a great republic divided into several states, some of which were monarchial, others mixed, some aristocratic, and others popular; but all corresponding with one another; all having the same basis of religion, though divided into several sects, and acknowledging the same principles of public and political equity, which were unknown to the other parts of the world.
>
> (*Le Siècle de Louis XIV*, II,1)

During the Enlightenment, Europe was therefore seen as a complex mechanism, but acknowledged as a unit; a space defined by various religious, and shared cultural, values and customs which differentiated it, anthropologically, from the other known parts of the world: America, Africa, and Asia.

Travels, commerce, identities

How did Europe acquire this self-awareness? It was possibly an effect of the Europeans' discovery of the American continent, which brought about a heightened awareness of the *other*, and of lands that may have been known but had not been travelled. As Montesquieu put it:

> The compass opened, if I may so express myself, the universe. Asia and Africa were found, of which only some borders were known; and America, of which we knew nothing.
>
> (*Spirit*, XXI, 2)

The compass was invented in China, a country "in between" by self-definition (*Zhongguo*, the Chinese name for their country, means "the land in the middle"), and a country which considers itself as continental: the sea, in Chinese culture, is viewed with suspicion, as evidenced in Marco Polo's report of the famous expedition by Qublai in Japan, and its disastrous outcome (*Travels*, Book III, 2). In Europe, the invention of the compass, together with that of paper and gunpowder, was received in a very different context, and the positive relation with the sea and with travel became instrumental in overcoming the prohibition on sailing beyond Gibraltar; the expression *Non plus ultra* ("nothing further beyond"), which features on the Spanish flag, became by paradox an emblem of the definitive liberation of Europe and its projection overseas, beyond the strictures of the lands which embrace the Mediterranean Sea. The Iberian Peninsula, excluded from Charlemagne's Europe, became the main actor in the discovery of the new continent to the west.

The movement from east to west was at the root of the formation of Europe, and echoed the movement of Ulysses in the myth, as he travelled in his search for his own self, finding it at the centre of the Mediterranean Sea. The ancient civilization travelled west, from Troy to Rome, as did Virgil's Aeneas, personification of the founding myth of the Roman Empire; both myth and empire being sponsored by Augustus. Virgil's *Aeneid* tells the story of the man who established a new descent and a new home in Italy, protected by his Asian household deities. Aeneas chose as his new land the peninsula which divides the Mediterranean Sea into two. The *Aeneid* revisits and strategically unifies the myth of Ulysses with that of Aeneas.

Sitting at the root of the new European literature, Dante too, in his prophetic and literary voyage, had to confront Ulysses the traveller, as the pagan archetype of his human experience and of his literature. Ulysses preceded both Aeneas and Dante's literary persona in the journey beyond death, but only the latter did it as a Christian poet and as a theologian. The medieval journeys westwards (and northwards for Saint Brendan the Navigator, one of the twelve apostles of Ireland) are products of the imagination and are marked by the prohibition of excessive curiosity. Ulysses himself would drown with his fellow travellers after five months of sailing because of his unbounded eagerness to learn what lies beyond the pillars of Hercules. The voyage of Dante's Ulysses – as of other travellers before Columbus – was one way only. Christopher Columbus, on the other hand, came back to share his acquired knowledge; such was his desire to do so that he enveloped his report in an oilskin and entrusted it to a large barrel of madeira in case his ship would sink in the gale that engulfed him on his first return from the Americas. In this gesture one may detect the perception of the sea as both peril and means of communication and salvation.[8] Columbus, perceived as the new Ulysses even in his own time, discovered the West Indies on the wings of Marco Polo, the great land traveller of centuries past. He had read Polo's *Book of the Marvels of the World* and was convinced that beyond the land he had just found lay that of the *Gran Chane* (Great Khan). His letter on the discovery of the Americas also indulges, through Polo's influence, in evoking the marvellous and the fantastic, even though it is in general based on an accurate and objective description of the new land.

Travels and close encounters with wondrous other worlds represented an existential metaphor in medieval literature. The Venetians and the Genoese established the first maritime empires in history. Even before Marco Polo and his father, merchants and religious people had travelled across the entire continent of Asia and described its ways, riches, and habits. When Columbus landed in San Salvador he was convinced he had touched the Indies, and not only because of Polo's accounts: before tackling the idea of having touched *otherness*, he may have preferred to imagine he had met his own self, and he would compare new and old through the lens of tradition.

The European states slowly acknowledged that the new lands were richer and bigger than the lands they already knew; that this *other* was different and that it would initiate a thorough cultural renovation. Europe, until then the only west, had discovered another west, and as it contemplated its central position in a Eurocentric expanded world (as it still remains today, to some extent) it also saw some of the key elements of its identity transferred westwards; and it feared this process – with an archetypical fear, rather than on the basis of analytic reasoning.

After the voyage to America by European explorers, the Mediterranean and Italy which lay at Europe's historic centre lost their central position:

> Italy was no longer the centre of the trading world; it was, if I may be permitted the expression, only a corner of the universe, and is so still. The commerce even of the Levant depending now on that of the great trading nations to both the Indies, Italy even in that branch can no longer be considered as a principal.
>
> (Montesquieu, *Spirit*, XXI, 21)

The dominance of northern Europe over the Mediterranean was consolidated, and Italy would soon lose the cultural pre-eminence it had enjoyed from the thirteenth to the sixteenth century, despite both regions being crucial, in a way, for the planning and success of the transoceanic voyage.

The travels eastwards of the Portuguese navigator also brought an encounter with an *other*, but one that could be neither totally colonized nor completely exploited commercially. Too much land, too many legends, and peoples, and too much history stood in the way of novelty. According to Montesquieu, the Barbarians (as much as the feared Tartars) "were commonly small nations, capable of being united" and then able "to make a great conquest in some southern empire"; by contrast, the savage nations "are dispersed in clans, which, for some particular reason, cannot be joined in a body" (*Spirit*, XVIII, 11).

The American so-called savages would pay dearly for their inability to organize themselves into a group, and would become a commodity to be exploited, as much as their own land which was turned into a commercial space not needing a link to an empire, or even a state:

> The Spaniards considered these new-discovered countries as the subject of conquest; while others, more refined in their views, found them to be

the proper subjects of commerce […]. Hence several nations have conducted themselves with so much wisdom, that they have given a kind of sovereignty to companies of merchants, who governing these far-distant countries only with a view to trade, have made a great accessary power, without embarrassing the principal state.

(*Spirit*, XXI, 21)

The space over the Ocean, west of western Europe, "following the sun" as Dante wrote,[9] suddenly materialized in a land, populated by animal and human prey. It became part of a Europe made up of warring nations, which discovered itself as part of a greater world:

A consequence of the discovery of America was the connecting of Asia and Africa with Europe; it furnished materials for a trade with that vast part of Asia known by the name of the East-Indies. Silver, that metal so useful as the medium of commerce, became now, as a merchandize, the basis of the greatest commerce in the world. *In fine*, the navigation to Africa became necessary, in order to furnish us with men to labour in the mines, and to cultivate the lands of America.

(*Spirit*, XXI, 21)

Europe's space was projected beyond the seas; sails and cannons became the essence of its dominance and its technical superiority in war and conquest. The silver, the goods, commerce and finance as well as capitalism became its winning grounds, as the *other* was reduced to a commodity for the ruling powers – which may also somehow explain the rationale of the preposterous debate as to whether or not the American indigenous peoples had a soul.

Sails and cannons

Conquests and explorations were made possible by the devastating and combined powers of sails and cannons.[10] The great Arabic and Asian empires were outflanked from behind, and as the Europeans sailed off in search of riches and of their own identity, they also discovered the definitive power of technologies in war, travel, and commerce.

Such technical superiority over time gave birth to modern physics, in turn originating from the new scientific method based on proof through experience that Galileo Galilei developed, and gave to his fellow Europeans as a revolutionary paradigm. Ptolemaic space was replaced with a new system based on geometrical and mathematical models retrieved from classical tradition but developed by Copernicus in the sixteenth century. As Gadamer pointed out,[11] during the seventeenth century the relationship between science and philosophy hit a crucial point and became both foundational for our culture and problematic. The whole cultural tradition and its wisdom, subdivided into branches and arts such as medicine, astronomy, philology, and rhetoric, had to contend with a new idea of what constituted knowledge. For the new branch of learning mechanical physics, Galileo devised the definition *mente concipio*, that is to say the science which studies movement as a pure conceptual abstraction. Through this science Galileo discovered the equations for a falling body moving from a situation, the fall of a body in an empty space, which cannot be observed in nature. The degree of abstraction and the ability to isolate the factors at work, as well as to establish their relations, were very innovative acquisitions which would inaugurate a new era in the relationships between mankind, the physical world, and its intelligence and representation. The scientific method replaced Renaissance philology and textual studies to which the rediscovery of Euclid, Archimedes, Diophantus and their interpretation must be credited. Mathematics, considered the ultimate rational method, replaced rhetoric and persuasion in an ideal intellectual hierarchy:

> Mathematics embraces the rules of logic, it relates to the very forms which shape knowledge not to the content of what is being said. As a consequence the very concept of reason (*logos-ratio*) changed: reason became the way to establish relations between facts, by comparing and counting quantities, whilst previously it consisted in the faculty of producing content. Abstracting from content to form made it possible for the critical methodology of science to be applied to all branches of learning, from medicine, to politics, to ethics and would be applied to erudition and philology as well. Baruch Spinoza even wrote an *Ethica more geometrico demonstrata*.
>
> (Stabile, 51)

Textual criticism would also elaborate its own scientific methodology, currently known as Lachmann's, which aims at reconstructing an author's text without interpretation (*sine interpretatione*), only by inference from the relationship between the manuscripts or printed books which had transmitted that text, organized and represented (even visually) as a family tree known as the *stemma codicum*.

European learning was divided up into zones, according to which of the two methodologies prevailed – the scientific or the philological; the former was better developed in the North, which was influenced to a lesser degree by Latin tradition and the Italian Renaissance, and became more open to the Reformation, the latter was livelier in southern, Latin and Romance Europe, which had been more largely affected by the Counter Reformation. Northern Europe would propel the Enlightenment, which was to be a (re)unifying force throughout Europe, signalling science as the origin and primary component of any form of learning. The French *Encyclopédie, ou Dictionnaire raisonné des sciences, des artes, et des métiers* would mark a turning point for the renewal of learning, and its classification:

As if it were a mechanical handbook the *Dictionnaire raisonné* presented knowledge as divided into simple elements. From a concept of learning as a body, which was inherited from Renaissance thought, modern thought represented it as a machine. Knowledge, however organized in units, is only bound by method: moving from simple elements one can combine different strategies to form a unity which is open to new acquisitions, where it is not content or quantity that matters, but rather the method through which single elements are assembled and knowledge constructed. Knowledge assumes therefore the nature of a work in progress, planned as a structure governed by a method but always susceptible of being expanded and enriched and—as the case may be—changed without limitations of time and space.

(Stabile 52)

Advances in science and technology led, as is well known, to the Industrial Revolution, when Europe's awareness of its values made another forward leap, and which also resulted in a deepening of the gap between the cultures of the sciences and those of the humanities.

Lay circles argued for Europe's cultural cohesion, based on its intellectuals and their institutions:

A republic of letters was insensibly established in Europe, in the midst of the most obstinate war, and the number of different religions. […]. The truly learned of every denomination have strengthened the bonds of this grand society of geniuses, which is universally diffused, and everywhere independent. This correspondence is still carried on, and proves one of the greatest comforts against the evils which ambition and politics scatter through the world.

(Voltaire, *Age of Louis XIV*, XXX)

It is probably not due to chance that the most convincing arguments in favour of the existence of a European identity came during the age of the Enlightenment; since in the balanced equilibrium devised by diplomats and politicians of the eighteenth century there was a special space for *les philosophes*. Such a space was described by reason, and no longer by power or religion as had been the case during the late Middle Ages. The European space became transnational: an ensemble of shared beliefs no longer pertaining to religion alone and not confined to a geographical space; the Republic of letters (*respublica literarum*) existed side by side with the Christian Republic (*respublica christiana*) and acquired a crucial role for Europe. Were it not for the fact that during the Middle Ages and the Renaissance there were already signs of a concept of Europe there would be grounds to argue that the idea of Europe belongs to modernity, and in particular to the age of the Enlightenment and of idealism, when its archetypes where revisited and reassessed in an ideal line harmoniously linking the Mediterranean to the north and antiquity to modernity.

When the first theorizations about its unique identity were being formulated, Europe was not a supranational system but a cultural common space guarded by and protecting *les philosophes*. Cosmopolitism coalesced around an idea and an ideal space, not a system, even though academies and cultural institutions formed that ideal intellectual circle which Dante had theorized in his *De Vulgari eloquentia*. In order to function, however, such a space has to rely on the relative stability of a political system (much as had happened in fifteenth-century Italy) and in the Enlightenment it was subjected to the instability caused by clashes between nations, conflicting interests, and political tensions.

The moment it hit the real world, the French Revolution would sweep away the *Ancien Régime* together with the European utopia that its spiritual founding fathers had believed in. If Europe consists of progress, change, and development (as Montesquieu argued in his *Lettres Persanes*) then the balance of powers cannot be static, otherwise the system will eventually crack. Modern Europe was born with the French Revolution, under the aegis of the inevitability of change, and the social influence and strength of its armies. Modern capitalism embraced the idea of Europe as a changing force.

The formula *liberté, égalité, fraternité* unified Europe in a transverse movement: for a prolonged instant the *philosophes* were deluded into thinking they led the process, but soon enough European citizens and intellectuals understood that their allegiances should follow their ideological convictions and social standing, not their geographical citizenship. The political and historical *querelle* (debate) opened by the French Revolution remains difficult to interpret to this day, and should be reassessed in light of the other, later, transverse and eventually national attempt at a radical uprising, the Bolshevik Revolution.

Europeans, especially after the October Bolshevik (or Socialist) Revolution of 1917, identify themselves with their political stance. The clash between states and national ideologies tended to prevail; the contrast between a Europe of the people and a Europe of the states, or regions and homelands, originated in the early twentieth century, although it feeds on ancient and medieval matter. Napoleon's attempt to unify Europe by force under French rule failed; it had a directly contrary historical effect, making the recognition of national states more urgent, as the histories of Germany and Italy demonstrate. Neither nation had participated to any significant extent in the colonial expansion which gained impetus with the first geographical discoveries and then with the Industrial Revolution. Their late and hurried industrialisation, and disorderly economic growth after unification would result in Nazi-Fascism and in the Second World War, the latest major tragedy in European history, a war which – as much as the First – had started as a European war but would soon extend to the rest of the world.

Time and catastrophe

The geopolitical and cultural spaces of Europe do not overlap; and any definition requiring such overlapping would be aborted by the fact that only in 1957 with the Treaty of Rome was a form of political unity achieved, nor can one speak of cultural unity across the entire region. In actual fact, as we saw, ideas of Europe first derived from a shared cultural awareness which ran from antiquity to the Enlightenment. It is effectively difficult to conceptualize Europe from within Europe. When one wants to "think of Europe in a clear and definite way, Europe itself dissolves, if one wants to acknowledge its unity, it fragments instantly" (Morin 21). This is

> the difficulty of thinking of a *unitas multiplex*, that is unity within multiplicity and multiplicity within unity, whilst at the same time thinking of identity as a combination of different identities. What makes European culture is not a synthesis of Judaic, Christian, Greek and Roman traditions—each of which had its own logic—but their dialogue with each other.
>
> (ibid)

"Each of which had its own logic", says Morin, and therefore we may add that each had its own time and space. European literature as seen by Curtius in his *European Literature and the Latin Middle Ages*[12] included both the (ancient) Mediterranean and the (modern) West – Greece and Rome, Paris, Madrid, and Vienna; that of an American comparatist like H. Bloom[13] was limited to modernity, excluded Dante and Chaucer and started from the sixteenth century. The Anglicist and comparatist Franco Moretti[14] centres on the big nation states and their relations from the sixteenth century onwards. Both Bloom's and Moretti's Europe appear constrained and narrow, even though Moretti does project it onto the European literary system. European literature does not fit into the constraints of defined nations alone, however interconnected they were; in particular if one considers that, unlike the hard sciences until not long ago, art does not proceed by exclusion of what is outdated, but through accumulation. A great Anglo-American poet of the last century argued that a writer should feel that:

> the whole of the literature of Europe from Homer and within it the whole of the literature of his own country has a simultaneous existence and composes a simultaneous order.
>
> (Eliot, 44)

Eliot was the most prominent representative of a humanities-oriented theory about literary tradition. It would, however, be difficult to deny that one of the great masterpieces of twentieth-century modernity, Joyce's *Ulysses*, represents in its matter (the book) the meeting point of tradition and the *avant garde*. The figure of Ulysses has marked new beginnings in western literature from Dante onwards, and often presents a crossing of the Greek space into the modern, western European space. As Joyce's *oeuvre* shows, in spite of its ostensibly constrained fictional settings, and as Eliot insisted and Curtius too argued, the time and space of European literatures could not be constrained by national boundaries and a stilted chronology:

> But for current literary history modern Europe does not begin until about 1500. This is as intelligent as if one were to promise a description of the Rhine, but only provided the section from Mainz to Cologne [...] The literature of "modern" Europe is as intermingled with that of the Mediterranean as if the Rhine had received its waters from the Tiber.
>
> (Curtius 10)

In actual fact, the minute one tries to define the space of European literature, it reveals its complex nature in terms of both time and place. If modern as well as contemporary European literature is a multifaceted system made up of a network of relations between differing units across time and space, the time of literature will have to account for the "simultaneous order" that Eliot conceived. Further, this will happen in every intellectual field, each being organized in a specific relation to time and space. Time and space are never objectively defined, and certainly not in Europe, which can be regarded, as Morin has argued, as a geographical concept, and thus as a space without borders.

Notes

1 Massimo Cacciari, *Geo-filosofia dell'Europa*, Milano, Adelphi, 1994.
2 Herodotus, *The Histories*, IV, 45; Isocrates, *Helen*, 51.
3 Chabod 29–30. Here, and wherever no English translation is cited, the translator is Nadia Cannata.
4 See R. Picchio, *Etudes littéraires slavo-romanes*, Firenze, Licosa editrice, 1978.
5 See *De Vulgari Eloquentiae*, I, 8
6 H. Lüdtke, *Die Entstechung romanischer Schriftsprachen*, in "Vox Romanica", 23 (1964), 3–21.
7 See Nos LXXXI, CXXXI, and CXXXVIII.
8 See Boitani.
9 Dante, *Inf.* XXVI.
10 See Cipolla.
11 See especially 10–11.
12 First published in 1948.
13 In his 1994 book *The Western Canon*.
14 In *La letteratura europea*, 1993.

2 Europe's time

Antiquity and modernity, tradition and innovation

In the same way as Europe's space is dynamic and subject to change, Europe's time has been evolving across the centuries. Concepts of time and periodization change within the history of ideas and ideologies, with the periodization of the history of Europe depending upon cultural perceptions and political events. What Aeschilus and Thycidides perceived as Europe had its core in Greece, Thrace, and the Hellespont and, due to the medieval transfer of culture and knowledge (*translatio studii*), travelled across the Mediterranean Sea. In literary terms perceptions of Europe develop across the three millennia discussed by Auerbach in his *Mimesis: the Representation of Reality in Western Literature*, or the 26 centuries – from Homer to Goethe – featuring in Curtius (op cit.), or in the twenty-eight centuries discussed by de Rougemont's *Vingt-huit siècles d'Europe* (1961).

Europe seen as an ensemble of nations is grounded in a variety of different principles presiding over social structures:

> Take ever so rapid a glance at this, and it strikes you at once as diversified, confused, and stormy. All the principles of social organization are found existing together within it; powers temporal, powers spiritual, the theocratic, monarchic, aristocratic, and democratic elements, all classes of society, all the social situations, are jumbled together, and visible within it; as well as infinite gradations of liberty, of wealth, and of influence. These various powers, too, are found here in a state of continual struggle among themselves, without any one having sufficient force to master the others, and take sole possession of society. [...].
>
> In the moral character, in the notions and sentiments of Europe, we find the same variety, the same struggle. Theocratic opinions, monarchical opinions, aristocratic opinions, democratic opinions, cross and jostle, struggle, become interwoven, limit, and modify each other.
>
> (Guizot 37–38)

This idea of Europe developed after the European exploration of America and developed further after the French Revolution. It is reflected in five centuries

DOI: 10.4324/9781003363323-2

of European literature: "The sixteenth century worked as a watershed – a barrier marking the separation from the past and from other continents – and only after this date did European literature acquire the daring inventiveness which is its characteristic feature" (Moretti *La letteratura* 817).

Whilst it is possible that the foundation of Europe's uniqueness lay with discovering and mixing with the "other" – *the association of the contraries* or the *vortex* as Morin put it – , this idea applies less elegantly to literature and culture. Europe's *vortex* is made of a *longue durée*, a continuity upset twice, by two *catastrophes* (the term is here used with its original meaning from Greek drama, i.e. the falling action leading to the tragic end). First the collapse of the Roman Empire, which laid the conditions for the emergence of otherness once a major political unity was broken, and later the exploration of America, when Europeans (still deluded in considering their lands as constituting the centre of the world) conceived of other continents as commodities to be exploited. The reconceptualization of temporality, which resulted from the double catastrophe explains why the articulation of Europe's history cannot be described by a single unilinear movement.

Up to the age of Cassiodorus (c. 490–c. 583), the separation between antiquity and modernity was only generational, a continuity at time describable by cycles, which is common to all societies based on agriculture; "modern becomes ancient and all that today is ancient was once modern" claimed Leopardi in his *Zibaldone* (10–12 October 1821). He echoed, albeit in a different context, the great Latin rhetorician Quintilian (c. 35–c. 95 CE.): *Nam et quae vetera nunc sunt fuerunt olim nova et quaedam sunt in usu perquam recentia* ("for words which now are old, once were new, and there are some words in use which are of quite recent origin") (VIII.3, 34).

Christian culture effected, in religious terms, the conceptual leap that brought the idea of antiquity to western culture: the antinomy or contrast between *Vetus* (Old) and *Novum* (New) *Testamentum* (Pact)[1] and the resolution of the old in the new marks a discontinuity between ancients and moderns, breaking for all subsequent ages the idea of time as a cycle linked to the natural world and to seasons, rather than to culture. The birth of Christ marks a turning point: everything that occurred before it is old, and all that comes after it is new.

The very idea of tradition (*traditio*) – that is the transmission to the next generations of something which clearly carries some value – would not have made much sense were it not grounded in the idea that a difference between past and present needed to be recognized and at the same time overcome and be reabsorbed in a new synthesis. The idea of tradition is at the root of the idea of linguistic *Thesauri*, and of the need for a canon of authors and texts regarded as intrinsically of value, and – of course – of the idea of what constitutes a classic", in other words which texts must be regarded as superior to others. Classics are taken out of time; to such an extent that their remoteness in time is an essential component of their value. For over one thousand years

European Latin culture was based upon a list of canonical authors to be read, studied at school, annotated, and thought upon according to a reading mode quite different from what is currently adopted: slow and deep and based on memory. Then, very few books were read, but they were read in great depth, as opposed to now, when we read many, quite indiscriminately.

Canon and tradition constitute for European culture a treasure secured from the ravages of time and transformation, as they shape a frame of mind, a paradigm through which the world is interpreted and a class of people, scholars, or *philosophi* (precursors of the *philosophes*) who are entrusted with the role of guardians of tradition and its riches, and of safeguarding it from the demands of the present and from change, even though in Europe one must always contend with change.

All this would not have resulted in the *longue durée* we know were it not for the crisis effected by the collapse of the Roman Empire, already perceived as such by contemporaries. When Cassiodorus (and before him Pope Gelasius) coupled *antiquus* with the term *modernus* (from the Latin *modo*, meaning "now") we observe the process through which the past was perceived as a value: *ad statum [...] pristinum [...] cuncta [...] revocare [...] ut [...] nostris temporibus videatur antiquitas decentius innovata* ("to the state [...] of the former [...] everything [...] to recall [...] so that [...] in our times antiquity may be seen more decently renewed") (*Variae* IV 51, 12; 202). Those who succeeded were praised as *antiquorum diligentissimus imitator, modernorum nobilissimus institutor* ("the most attentive imitator of the ancients, the noblest instructor of the moderns") (*Variae* IV 51, 1; 201).

The first mark of discontinuity from the past signals the birth of Europe's time; the Christian renovation embraces the pagan other and establishes a tradition on this foundation; the collapse of the old Empire and of its monuments assumes a model of time based on consciousness of what had been and is no more; a new concept of absolute time runs along natural time, made of a fluent sequence of old and new. Classical antiquity was opposed to modernity in all cultural expressions, literature included, where ancient culture had no use in medieval modern times. Ancient and modern, according to context and social situation, could both be carriers of values or objects of a critical assessment of values.

For the first time in western culture the issue of how to build a tradition out of a fracture and how to partially recoup what had been refused became urgent. The operation was perceived as possible since this is how the new religion was established, with a renewed pact which did not dissolve the *old* but established a *new* one. The Old Testament was interpreted allegorically (*allegory* comes from *allon argoreuein*, to say differently), as it was supposed that its letter contained various meanings and also that the stories of old prefigured what was to come, the new.

The texts, the only true image and replica of the world according to medieval culture, were used again and again, outside of a temporal sequence, out of any context, every time new reader-interpreters wished to interrogate them to give answers to current issues. Texts were used not *iuxta propria principia*, in their own right, but to signify something else, a development of the new from the old. European tradition is constituted by that synthesis of new and old, and, after the first catastrophe, the Church's titanic efforts to embrace in its bosom the *societas gentilium* (the pre-Christian pagans deserving of salvation) and allow it to be part of the time of salvation, in itself ahistorical and based on the birth of Christ the Saviour, from which time started again, hurtling towards the Day of Judgement.

The impossibility for Medieval culture to represent antiquity as history must be due to the Church Fathers' violent reappropriation of the pagan past as the foundations of this renewed present – a political form of history, it could be argued. As a consequence, European cultural history would be characterized by its unique way of looking at the conflicting arguments of tradition vs innovation, that have repeatedly and constantly been pitched against each other. Successive renaissances would mark the value and relevance of classical culture, of its myths and symbols, as well as, at the same time, the need to interpret the past in its own right, and to disenfranchize it from the Church.

Perched on the shoulders of giants in search of the self

The apparent stillness of medieval time is related to the slow pace of political and economic change in Europe from the fifth to the twelfth century. At a time when politics and economics were regaining their impetus, philosophers were also rediscovering Aristotle's philosophy, translated from the Greek by Arab scholars, and the dialectical method. The effects of such changes would be manifested in all fields: philosophy, literature, and architecture – as well as agriculture, where new techniques were developed and adopted to everyone's benefit.

The idea that culture is grounded in tradition was complemented by the discovery of the merits of innovation. The dialectical method was also applied to the relationship between ancients and moderns, furnishing an idea of progress along the line of time: the ancient works (both classical and Christian) were regarded as venerable and as comprising a tradition that should be assiduously studied and honoured; the moderns, however dwarfed by their ancestors' stature, if perched on their shoulders should be able to see more and to cast their gaze further. As John of Salisbury wrote:

> *possimus plura eis et remotiora videre, non utique proprii visus acumine aut eminentia corporis, sed quia in altum subvehimur et extollimur magnitudine gigantea*

> We may see more and farther than our predecessors not because we have keener vision or greater height, but because we are lifted up and borne aloft on their gigantic stature.

(III.4 167)

In Medieval Europe, intellectuals challenged Aristotle's law of non-contradiction, the comparison and confrontation between ancients and moderns – *sic et non*, yes and no; the acknowledgement that it constituted a methodological issue allowed a process of self-identification to be initiated. The encounter with other cultures, Arabs in Sicily and Spain, and Jews throughout Europe during the twelfth century, presented new stimuli and made available previously lost fundamental texts in philosophy, science, and culture in general, which Byzantine Europe did not have any knowledge of or interest in. Taking advantage of inventions and contraptions devised by other civilizations and only partially used in their places of origin (the compass, the printing press, gunpowder etc.) became one of Europe's distinct features.

Contact with the Arabs, a far superior urban culture (when medieval Rome had less than 30,000 citizens, Cordoba had around ten times as many), was not only of relevance to culture. Arabs controlled the Mediterranean and had pushed Charlemagne's empire onto the continent, whilst forcing Europeans to engage in a process of self-identification. For a long time, Arabs called the Crusaders simply "Franks", a unitary group of "others".

The action of the *Chanson de Roland*, which appeared at the start of the era of the Crusades and of Europe's expansion overseas, happens in the very land that had witnessed the peaceful and fertile coexistence between Arabs, Christians, and Jews. Written around three hundred years after the events it narrates, the *Chanson de Roland* elaborated on a defeat and transformed it, through storytelling, into a victory. Roland is killed, but Charlemagne will win and vindicate him. The past is reviewed to serve the present (perhaps the launch of another crusade to liberate Spain from the Arabs) and this established a paradigm still working in contemporary culture for popular epic narrations (even in films, as in Hollywood's westerns), which entailed the creation of a myth in order to move the public into action. As St. Augustine had already argued, *ut aliquid agat est flectendus auditor*: "the listener must be emotionally moved in order for him to act" (*De Doctrina* IV 19).

Through the clash with the *other* and the making of an enemy, the *Chanson de Roland* and romance epic in general – soon followed by retellings of the Arthurian legends – unified Europe in myth, imagery, and even place-names, and the local names given to Charles and the paladins chart a renewed cultural geography of Europe. The *Chanson de Roland* invited listeners to acknowledge their own identity; "the pagans are wrong, Christians are right" claimed the poet, repeatedly. European merchants, knights, and adventurers would need nothing further to move themselves in pursuit and appropriation of the riches of the world. The Crusades would happen in rapid succession, and in 1204 even Constantinople, the capital of the lost Christian Empire, would fall into the hands of the Crusaders' armies, which proved to be highly destructive and predatory. With this, Europe moved against the very symbol of its continuity, the Roman rulers of an Empire which had proven unable to sustain social or economic change.

The knights from Charlemagne's legends became adventurers in search of their own selves: from Perceval to Wagner's Perzeval, from Dante to Joyce, European literature and culture identified the voyage as a founding metaphor (again extracted from the flow of time) to understand what is the sense of our existence. The Christian is a *viator*, a traveller not just on a journey to the afterlife, but in search for a meaning to be found in this world in order to become deserving of what comes after it. Such a journey, being an experience of the self, also implies a particular kind of time: Dante is at the same time Ulysses and Aeneas, Moses and Christ, but most of all he is the former *stilnovista* love poet turned moral poet and exiled from Florence in 1302. The time of the self, starting from the time of St. Augustine, many centuries before Proust, is a time in its own right, with a pace of its own, independent of the actual succession of events which normally marks the passing of time.

Re-birth and the complexity of time

John of Salisbury's statement has a humanistic overtone, even though it was only with the invention of philology and textual criticism – aimed at retrieving the truth of ancient texts and their language via the study of the errors in their transmission – that the perception of a historical as opposed to an absolute time was perfected, at least in as far as possible, given that (as twentieth century science demonstrated) the observer always influences the object observed. The objective of achieving a reliable interpretation of ancient texts thanks to a critical method which considers them in their historical context (and therefore in their own time) gave birth to Humanism and to a Re-naissance (rebirth) from the dark ages, one quite different from earlier renaissances known to European history (the Carolingian and twelfth century renaissances), which, too, were characterized by the desire to preserve and value ancient texts and traditions.

Petrarch, one of the founders of Humanism and philology, valued ancient times because they were opposed to a difficult present, as he claimed in his letter to posterity, written, of course, in Latin:

> *Incubui unice, inter multa, ad notitiam vetustatis, quoniam michi semper etas ista displicuit; ut, nisi me amor carorum in diversum traheret, qualibet etate natus esse semper optaverim, et hanc oblivisci, nisus animo me aliis semper inserere.*

(XVIII, 1, 11–12)

I dwelt especially upon antiquity, for our own age has always repelled me, so that, had it not been for the love of those dear to me, I should have preferred to have been born in any other period than our own. In order to forget my own time, I have constantly striven to place myself in spirit in other ages.

(Petrarch, Robinson (trans) 64)

Petrarch and the humanists established a critical method which put into question texts of crucial political importance such as the *Donation of Constantine*, which had served as guarantor of the secular power of the Roman Church throughout the Middle Ages and was revealed as false by Lorenzo Valla. Humanistic philology aimed at revealing the actual truth of classical texts independently of any allegorical interpretation of their letter.

Italian Humanism and its Renaissance made sure that the whole of Europe acknowledged that it was rooted in classical tradition. They existed at the foundations of a transnational movement which developed in different times and modes in European countries, and for the first time, as Machiavelli showed, the countries of Europe were seen as distinct and opposed within a single European identity. Such identity served the conflict with "others" and lay at the base of the Enlightenment, another transnational European cultural movement.

Philology, textual criticism, and the Renaissance established the renewed and revived European culture, and moving from previous forms of re-birth contributed to keeping alive the consideration of antiquity, to the point of refusing the *hic et nunc*, the here and now, in favour of a nostalgic desire to be elsewhere, which can be found from Petrarch onwards. Modernity could scarcely ever win in Europe – even in Napoleon's times, and in spite of attempts to progress and unify Europe under a new allegiance – the dominant style across the continent was neo-classical, a new way of re-using the antique, which followed countless other reuses of antiquity since Charlemagne's *Renovatio Romani Imperii*, or Renovation of the Roman Empire.

The idea of the *avant garde* itself was reiterated by European intellectuals so often that it became a category *per se*, and it stems from a culture steeped in tradition. T.S. Eliot claimed that literature had a value as the crucible and meeting point between past and present:

This historical sense, which is a sense of the timeless as well as of the temporal and of the timeless and of the temporal together, is what makes a writer traditional. And it is at the same time what makes a writer most acutely conscious of his place in time, of his contemporaneity.

(44)

The times of Europe (continuous, cyclic, absolute, historical, functional) constitute a complex system, intertwining and defining different points of view.

Time and progress

In the dynamics between time as such and progress, European intellectuals played a specific role as did humanistic culture by acquiring a social function that was strictly secular. The idea of progress as part of the relation between past and present became one of the characteristic features of European civilization, in contrast to others. Montesquieu understood the extent to which this conception of time was organic (and specific) to Europe's culture:

> Nobody likes to be poorer than he who is his immediate inferior. You may see at Paris a man with sufficient to live on till the end of the world, labouring constantly, and running the risk of shortening his days, to scrape together, as he says, a livelihood.
>
> (241)

The idea of an orderly passing of time collapsed, together with the political order upon which Voltaire's Europe was founded: if Europe was progress, development, and change, it was also necessary for time to gain pace and dynamism and became quicker and projected like an arrow, whilst progress became the new myth in the collective imaginary, as a new, creative, and symbolic dimension of the social world.

The universal expositions from the late nineteenth century brought together the public of the big metropolises and encouraged them to marvel at the magnificent future lying ahead for humanity. The ruling and intellectual classes marked the period preceding the First World War as a *Belle époque*, a time when progress seemed unstoppable and irreversible.

The First World War, the Soviet Revolution and the rise of the United States on the world stage would reveal an inner crisis in the system, which the American industrial model and the rise of mass culture had already signalled. Technological and scientific advancement is not infinite and does not cancel time, which is to be considered as the meeting point between its perception by the subject and the general social perception of the merits of its passing. Subjectivity and objectivity dilate it in unforeseeable ways, and analogy sometimes results in individual perceptions overruling the natural chronological sequence of events.

Europe's cultural memory and its tradition were considered by humanist intellectuals as an inheritance to be guarded from the assaults of the masses, seen as the new barbarians, and from the power of the present time over history and its memory:

> There is one fact which, whether for good or ill, is of utmost importance in the public life of Europe at the present moment. This fact is the accession of the masses to complete social power. As the masses, by definition, neither should nor can direct their own personal existence, and still less rule society in general, this fact means that actually Europe is suffering from the greatest crisis that can afflict peoples, nations, and civilisation. Such a crisis has occurred more than once in history. Its characteristics and its consequences are well known. So also is its name. It is called the rebellion of the masses.
>
> (Ortega y Gasset 11)

To barbarize is generally intended as the process due to which a spiritual situation of high value is slowly forced to recede by forces belonging to a lower order, and such lower order are a multitude, a social mass:

> Barbarisation may be defined as a cultural process whereby an attained condition of high value is gradually overrun and superseded by elements of lower quality.
>
> (Huizinga 212)

The crisis of Europe is therefore to be understood chiefly as a crisis of cultural tradition and values, in particular of humanistic culture, as generally perceived by intellectuals during the first half of the twentieth century. From their point of view, it entailed the loss of the unity of a culture in favour of the dissolution of its soul into that pastiche of time and space typical of contemporary urban/ metropolitan civilizations. It is an awareness often associated with a form of terror, which unites – notwithstanding their differences – Proust, Joyce, Thomas Mann, Hoffmansthal, and many others.

If one thinks back to the great catastrophe marking the end of antiquity, one recognizes that society may die again because it died once. A renewed and profound sentiment of uneasiness once more ran through European culture, as it had a couple of centuries before with the rise of the Enlightenment. The nostalgia resulting in the actual pain at the loss of a common home and a perceived unity manifested itself as a private, cultural, religious sentiment and became somehow a collective marker of European identity: *nostalgia*, *nostalgija*, *spleen*, *Sehnsucht*, *saudade* were variously articulated in all arts (think of the scream and rage of expressionism), to signify the loss of identity of the European intellectual.

The metropolis appeared as an indistinct mass which produced neither culture nor distinction, but only confusion and massification. Thus the capitalist paradigm, triumphant both economically and anthropologically, and in itself an original European invention, also shows its own limitations for both individuals and societies. Ways to seek ease from such disquiet, inbuilt in the western idea of civilization, were encountered at the end of the nineteenth and beginning of the twentieth centuries in Freudian Vienna, which sat at the very heart of Europe.

Freud forced Europe to speak to itself and deal with the *Un-behagen* (disquiet) resulting from being a society in constant opposition with its fathers, forced to change and progress constantly and to contend with the resultant *Un-heimlich* (the un-familiar – the uncanny – that is therefore frightening). Freud revealed Europe's limits, embedded in its self, and gave the world, together with a new therapy, a different conception of reason.

A new catastrophe?

Freudian psychoanalysis and Einstein's relativism as well as Heisenberg's uncertainty principle became pillars of philosophical thought and framed the perspective through which European history was addressed. In order to understand Europe's destiny, its history (conceived of as human history *tout court*) was scrutinized in every detail in numerous publications. Oswald Spengler's *The Decline of the West* (1918) was the first such publication, as it claims:

> In this book is attempted for the first time the venture of predetermining history, of following the still untravelled stages in the destiny of a Culture, and specifically of the only Culture of our time and on our planet which is actually in the phase of fulfilment—the West-European-American.
>
> (3)

How are cultures and the historical contexts in which they flourish born, how do they grow and then decline? According to Spengler,

> The means whereby to identify dead forms is Mathematical Law. The means whereby to understand living forms is Analogy. By these means we are enabled to distinguish polarity and periodicity in the world [...]. It is, and has always been, a matter of knowledge that the expression-forms of world-history are limited in number, and that eras, epochs, situations, persons are ever repeating themselves true to type.
>
> (4)

Thus, his theme

> expands into the conception of a morphology of world history, of the world-as-history in contrast to the morphology of the world-as-nature that hitherto has been almost the only theme of philosophy.
>
> (5)

The idea was to provide a structure for time, moving from the present age and its problems, in order to be able to comprehend history. However, new paradigms were being created on the other side of the Atlantic, often providing an anti-historic, analogical model.

The contrast with American culture compelled a new vision of Europe as the seat and origin of an ideal West, embracing all of the culture that it had generated. Mass communications and their spread had endangered its position as an elite culture, and the political developments of the 1930s – the rise of Fascism, Nazism, and Communism – alarmed liberal culture as they seemed to signal an imminent catastrophe, effected by the victory and unchecked power of the masses. The only seminal essay devoted to European literature, that of Curtius, was devised and written in such an atmosphere. It aims at applying to literature a structural historicism open to phenomenology, whereby it is possible to produce a morphology of basic "forms" which are repeated through twenty-six centuries of literature in Europe.

John Huizinga identified the crisis of humanistic culture as the *Shadow of Tomorrow*, embracing partially the arguments put forward by Spengler and Ortega y Gasset, the theoretician of the *Revolt of the Masses* (1930). A society based on agriculture and craftmanship, which set limits one could refer to and which provided the chance to recognize one's identity, gave way to a "passive society" which, even in sport, encouraged watching as opposed to acting, and where words and action tended to reproduce models rather than provide new ones. Such change – argued Huizinga in the first chapter of his book – lead to the atrophy of a whole series of intellectual functions.

The conservative critique of contemporary society in Europe became defensive in its fear of homogenization and refused to negotiate with the new cultural system and to embrace whatever positive qualities it may have had, thus providing the foundation of a structural diffidence towards the new times and the mass communications they initiated.

Novalis represented, once again, the underlying spiritual force of European culture, in the same way as he had interpreted the general uneasiness with eighteenth-century rationalism:

> Those were beautiful, magnificent times, when Europe was a Christian land, when one Christianity dwelled on this civilized continent, and when one common interest joined the most distant provinces of this vast spiritual empire. Without great worldly possessions one sovereign governed and unified the great political forces [...] How happily everyone could complete their earthly labors, since these holy men had safeguarded them a future life, forgave every sin, explained and erased every blackspot in this life.

("Christianity or Europe" 61)

The only positive response in 1930s Germany came from Walter Benjamin:

> The authenticity of a thing is the essence of all that is transmissible from its beginning, ranging from its substantive duration to its testimony to the history which it has experienced. Since the historical testimony rests on the authenticity, the former, too, is jeopardized by reproduction when substantive duration ceases to matter. And what is really jeopardized when the historical testimony is affected is the authority of the object [...].

> [. . .] The technique of reproduction detaches the reproduced object from the domain of tradition. By making many reproductions it substitutes a plurality of copies for a unique existence. And in permitting the reproduction

to meet the beholder or listener in his own particular situation, it reactivates the object reproduced. These two processes lead to a tremendous shattering of tradition which is the obverse of the contemporary crisis and renewal of mankind. Both processes are intimately connected with the contemporary mass movements.

(221)

[...] But the instant the criterion of authenticity ceases to be applicable to artistic production, the total function of art is reversed. Instead of being based on ritual, it begins to be based on another practice – politics.

(224)

A return journey

In Europe Tocqueville first and later Benjamin provided very acute analyses of the impact of democracy and mass media on cultural life. European intellectuals, however, seemed unable to take such awareness a step forward. In the United States on the other hand, in a land much freer from the constraints of tradition, tradition and rituals were reanalyzed and contextualized in a new system where the "other" became organically part of the very idea of the nation, as had once been the case in Europe. Cultural and linguistic contact, and the challenge of meeting different cultures had a positive effect in early medieval Europe too, when, after the collapse of the Roman Empire, discontinuity effected change. The same did not happen in the Eastern part of the Empire, as Byzantium remained locked in its Roman identity. But in the present day, the idea that Europe has to defend a presumed unitary cultural identity seems to challenge what had made it modern and diverse. The United States of America is now the land where diversity and European identities have become the archetypes of a new industrial and media culture.

The melting pot is the image chosen to signify America's cultural identity, and it is also used to represent a metaphor of the new urban culture. In the same way as city museums opened private collections to the community, the Great or Universal Expositions of the late nineteenth century extended the same principle to goods and to a worldly scale.[2] The United States appeared as the metropolis of a capitalism that offered the whole of human history as merchandise ready for consumption.

According to Franco Moretti the forms of literature follow the development of capitalism and its ideology:

In an extraordinary complicity between social phenomenon and literary form, therefore, advertising and the stream of consciousness pursue and implicate one another throughout *Ulysses*. The former is the inexhaustible transmitter of the capitalist metropolis; the latter, the receiver that captures and organizes fluctuating stimuli [...] Stream—fields. Waves—states. [---] It is the world of the great "Perhaps".

(*Modern Epic* 135–137)

This looks like an upended version of what actually happened during the twentieth century, as literature gave way to the culture of mass media and the new west took pre-eminence over the old. Words have become images, stimuli, desires, commodities, publicity, a yearning for novelty; the new media – radio, television, internet – have produced an ever-growing impetus for the production of news and a new anthropology of fictitious humanity.

Alberto Abruzzese argued that, with the invention of moving pictures, Hollywood took possession of the structural mechanisms of European literary discourse, as later described by Curtius (*European Literature*). Georges Polti elaborated a brilliant synthesis of figures and dramatic situations of the European narrative imagination, which classified by type the entire treasury of the ancient and modern European literary tradition, so as to furnish a structural framework to create new texts and original narrative plots. Polti's corpus acquired the function of a narrative storehouse for the American cultural industry. According to Polti:

The literary *topoi* of classical literature were transferred as stereotypes of mass culture and of cinematic language and the urban experience of Paris and London travelled to New York [...] Cultural industry became the laboratory transforming mitteleuropean and avangarde [*sic*] European qualities in the quantities required by mass culture. It could be argued that the entire process served to confirm Benjamin's theory about the loss of aura in art as technological advancements emphasized reproducibility, whilst quality is replaced by quantity.

(44)

The world unified under the aegis of the American collective imagination as European roots grew weaker, both for historical reasons (racial laws and the migration of most of democratic Jewish culture to the States) and due to the prevailing American industrial model.

When the desire for innovation and the sense of an ever growing plurality of possibilities, as well as the idea that human beings are indeterminate entities open to a variety of possible realities, took ground and met with cybernetics and the world of computers, a new virtual time and space that would subdue all known times and places was created. U-topia – a place not defined in space – and *utopia* defined as a desire for an unattainable hope became blurred. Virtual time and virtual space challenged the very existence of a specific and historical European space that could be described or defined with any precision. Such a space was at risk to be the land of nostalgia, where lost roots may be found, to be sold as goods, for tourism or other merchandise.

It may be possible to recover some space between utopia and nostalgia wherein to identify Europe as a unique and complex system of relations, which the virtual computer networks are unable to match. In the vital relation between past, present, and future, Novalis and Benjamin found a point of encounter. Novalis claimed that

> Even the present cannot at all be understood without the *past* and without a high degree of education—saturation with the highest products, the purest spirit of the age and of the past, and a digestion of this, from what source the human prophetic view arises, which the historian, the active, idealistic person who works with the data of history can as little do without.
>
> ("Last Fragments" 156)

whilst the revolutionary Benjamin revealed that:

> no fact that is a cause is for that very reason historical. It became historical posthumously, as it were, though events that may be separated from it by thousands of years. A historian who takes this as his point of departure stops telling the sequence of events like the beads of a rosary. Instead, he grasps the constellation which his own era has formed with a definite earlier one. Thus, he establishes a conception of the present as the 'time of the now' which is shot through with chips of Messianic time.
>
> ("Theses" 263)

In other words, if the current trend seems to force Europe to sever links, or at least to mark a distance from its roots,[3] such a process would result in an amputation of its identity and of its historical significance, a solution that in the long run never does pay off. Probably, as has been suggested, its deep roots in antiquity could put it back into play for its value as an archetype, in particular in a historical period like the present, in which mass culture and computer language seem to reinvent founding myths rather than transmit and divulge them.

Maybe it is time to give up a narrative of decadence and understand from without the significance and function of tradition and of European culture. A critique of tradition and of the intellectuals who built it are part of a critique of Europe, given the central role culture had in the building of a European identity. A new beginning is needed, and perhaps it is being heralded; a beginning in which Europe is not at the centre, but rather one of the parts making up a new system in which different ideas of Europe can coexist. As Trubeckoj pointed out, we need to understand that "neither 'I', nor anyone else is the navel of the earth, all peoples and cultures are equal and nobody is superior […] no culture exists without borrowing from other cultures, and borrowing implies no abnormality" (vii–viii).

This would be the exact opposite of the "Fortress Europe" evoked by Hitler at the time of one of Europe's most devastating destructions, a destruction that could be explained in Morin's words:

Anything that simplifies the idea of Europe—idealization, abstraction, or reduction—mutilates it. Europe is a complex item ("complexus" in Latin means "woven together") and its main feature is to bring together without confusion diversity and to associate contraries. We must understand the complexity that is hidden behind the word "Europe".

(101)

The reassessment of Europe's tradition has only just begun; it is now time to start to compare it with other traditions and look at history also through the lens of gender, in order to enable us to understand what significance a European culture might have for present day Europeans, and for future citizens of Europe – culture being the continent's only unifying factor in its long history, as Braudel had argued. To reassess one's own culture and to find its roots, moving from the present towards the past, might be the condition enabling us to appreciate our present (the *hic et nunc*) and to check it against the relation between culture and politics.

Today's difficult moment may also prove fascinating. An old system is gone, but something new whose identity needs to be designed is coming, provided that multiplicity and diversity are to be preserved and identities are not imposed by ways of war or violence. The twentieth century, a most critical period in the history of Europe, finished in a way far too similar to how it started: even the Balkans, theatre of the last European war, are burning again, and ideas or culture have proven unable to influence in any positive way the course of events. In order to start a new life, Europe must forget herself and her memories, as Goethe's Mephistofeles taught: "for all that comes to be, deserves to perish wretchedly (161)."[4]

Notes

1 The translation of *Testamentum*, or "pact", as "Testament" is part of the history of Biblical translations.
2 See A. Abruzzese, "La casa della bellezza", *Critica del testo*, I/1, 1998, 591–603.
3 Tocqueville, in *De la démocratie en Amérique*, identified Europe through its link to its past.
4 Goethe, *Faust*, Part I, Scene 3.

Bibliography

Abruzzese, A. "La casa della bellezza." *Critica del testo*, I, 1998, pp. 591–603.

Aeschylus. *Persians*. Vol. I. Translated by H.W. Smyth. Cambridge: Harvard University Press, 1926.

Auerbach, E. *Mimesis. Dargestellte Wirklichkeit in der abendländischen Literatur*. Bern: Francke, 1946.

Augustine of Hippo. *De Doctrina Christiana*. Translated by R.P.H. Green. Oxford: Clarendon Press, 1995.

———. *The City of God (De Civitate Dei) XI–XXII*. Translated by William Babcock. New York: New City Press, 2013.

Benjamin W. "The Work of Art in the Age of Mechanical Reproduction." In *Illuminations. Essays and Reflections*. Translated by H. Zohn. New York Schocken Books, 1968, pp. 217–252.

Benjamin, W. "Theses on the Philosophy of History." In *Illuminations. Essays and Reflections*. Translated by H. Zohn. New York: Schocken Books, 1968, pp. 253–264.

Bloom, H. *The Western Canon: The Book and School of the Ages*. San Diego, CA: Harcourt Brace, 1994.

Boitani, Piero. *L'ombra di Ulisse:* figure di *un mito*. Bologna: il Mulino, 1992.

Cacciari, M., *Geo-filosofia dell'Europa*. Milano: Adelphi, 1994.

Cassiodorus. *Cassiodorus The Variae: The Complete Translation*. Translated by M.S. Bjornlie. Oakland: University of California Press, 2019.

Chabod, F. *Storia dell'idea di Europa*. Bari: Laterza, 1961.

Cipolla, C.M. *Guns and Sails in the Early Phase of European Expansion. 1400–1700*. London: Collins, 1965.

Curtius, Ernst Robert. *European Literature and the Latin Middle Ages*. Translated by W.R. Trask. London: Routledge & Kegan Paul, 1953.

Alighieri, Dante. *La Commedia secondo l'antica Vulgata*. Edited by G. Petrocchi. Firenze: Le Lettere, 1994.

———. "Inferno." In *The Divine Comedy of Dante Alighieri. The Italian Text with a Translation in English Blank Verse and a Commentary by C. Langdon*, 3 vols. Cambridge: Harvard University Press, 1918.

———. *De Vulgari Eloquentiae*. Translated by Steven Botterill. Cambridge: Cambridge University Press, 1996.

———. "Monarchia." In *Dante, Monarchia*. Translated by Prue Shaw. Cambridge: Cambridge University Press, 1995.

———. *The Divine Comedy of Dante Alighieri*. Translated by C. Langdon. Cambridge, MA: Harvard University Press, 1918.

Eliot, T.S. "Tradition and the Individual Talent." In *The Sacred Wood*. London: Methuen, 1920, pp. 47–59.

Encyclopédie, ou Dictionnaire raisonné des sciences, des arts, et des métiers. By Denis Diderot and Jean le Rond d' Alembert. Paris: Le Breton, Durand, Briasson, Antoine David, 1751–1772.

Gadamer, H.G. *L'Eredita dell'Europa*. Translated by F. Cuniberto. Torino: Einaudi, 1991.

von Goethe, Johann Wolfgang. *Goethe's Faust*. Translated by Walter Kaufmann. New York: Anchor, 1961.

Guizot, F. *General History of European Civilization*. Translated by C.S. Henry. New York: D. Appleton and Co., 1846.

Hegel, G.W.F. *Lectures on the Philosophy of World History*. Translated by Peter C. Hodgson and Robert F. Brown. Volume 1. Oxford: Clarendon Press, 2011.

Herodotus. *Herodotus: With an English Translation*. Translated by A.D. Godley. London: William Heineman, 1920.

Horace. *Epistles*. Translated by C. Macleod. Rome: Edizioni dell'Ateneo, 1986.

Huizinga, J. *In the Shadow of Tomorrow; a Diagnosis of the Spiritual Distemper of Our Time*. Translated by J. Huizinga. London: William Heinemann, 1936.

"John of Salisbury." *Metalogicon*. Translated by D. McGarry, Berkeley: University of California Press, 1955.

Leopardi, Giacomo. "Zibaldone di Pensieri." In *Pensieri di varia filosofia e di bella letteratura*. Firenze: Le Monnier, 1921.

Machiavelli, N. "Art of War." In *The Works of Famous Nicolas Machiavel, Citizen and Secretary of Florence*. Translated by Henry Neville. London: Printed for J.S., 1675.

———. "Discourses on the First Decade of Livy." In *The Works of Famous Nicolas Machiavel, Citizen and Secretary of Florence*. Translated by Henry Neville. London: Printed for J.S., 1675.

Machiavelli, N. *The Prince by Nicolo Machiavelli*. Translated by W.K. Marriot. London: J.M. Dent-Dutton, 1908.

Matvejevic, P. *Mediterranean: A Cultural Landscape*. Berkeley: University of California Press, 1999.

Migne, J.P. *Patrologia Latina* 96. Paris: Garnier 1879.

Montesquieu, Ch.-L. de Secondat. *Persian Letters*. Translated by John. Davidson, London: Privately Printed, 1891.

———. "The Spirit of the Laws." In *The Complete Works of M. de Montesquieu, Translated from the French*. London: T. Evans and W. Davis, 1777.

Moretti, F. "La letteratura europea." In *Storia d'Europa I: L'Europa oggi*. Torino: Einaudi, 1993.

———. *Modern Epic. The World System from Goethe to Garcia Marquez*. Translated by Q. Hoare, London: Verso, 1996.

Morin, E. *Pensée l'Europe*. Paris: Gallimard, 1987.

Novalis [Friedrich von Hardenberg]. "Christianity or Europe. A Fragment." In *The Early Political Writings of the German Romantics*. Edited and translated by Frederick C. Beiser. Cambridge: Cambridge University Press, 1999, pp. 59–80.

———. "Last Fragments." In *Philosophical Writings*. Translated by M.M. Stoljar. Albany: State University of New York Press, 1997, pp. 153–166.

Ortega y Gasset, J. *The Revolt of the Masses*. New York: Norton, 1932.

Petrarch. *Senilium rerum libri, I fragmenta dell'epistola Ad Posteritatem di Francesco Petrarca*. Edited by L. Refe. Messina: Università di Messina, 2014.

―――. *Petrarch The First Modern Scholar and Man of Letters*. Translated by James Harvey Robinson. 2nd edn. New York: G.P. Putnam, 1914.

Picchio, R. *Etudes littéraires slavo-romanes*. Firenze: Licosa editrice, 1978.

Polo, Marco. *The Travels of Marco Polo*. Translated and Edited by H. Yule and H. Cordier. New York: Dover, 1993.

Polti, G. "Europa America: Andata e ritorno." In *Progetto Europa*. Roma, n.p., 1991.

Quintillian, Marcus Fabius. *Institutio Oratoria*. Translated by Harold Edgeworth Butler. London: W. Heinemann, 1922.

de Rougemont, Denis. *Vingt-huit siècles d'Europe*. Paris: Payot, 1961.

Spengler, Oswald. *The Decline of the West*. Translated by C.F. Atkinson. London: Allen & Unwin, 1926–29.

Stabile G. "Identità e diversità." In *Progetto Europa*. Roma, n.p., 1991.

de Tocqueville, A. "De la démocratie en Amérique." In *Œuvres, II*. Edited by A. Jardin, J-C. Lamberti and J.T. Schleifer. Paris: Gallimard, 1992.

Trubeckoj, N. *L'Europa e l'umanità*. Translated by Milan Olga Strada. Aspis Edizioni, 2021.

"Voltaire [Francois Marie Arouet]." *Essais sur les Moeurs Et L'Esprit des Nations*. n.p., n.p., 1773.

―――. *The Age of Louis XIV*. Translated by M.P. Pollack. London: Dent-Dutton, 1961.

Index

national states, recognition of 17
nostalgia 29, 31, 33–34
Novalis, Friedrich von Hardenberg
31, 34

Oath of Strasbourg 9
oceans 5
October Bolshevik Revolution
(1917) 17, 28
Old Testament 23
old/new dichotomy 22–25, 27, 29
Ortega y Gasset, J. 31
others: America as 14; and the
Chanson de Roland 25; mixing
with 22

paper 12
Paris 18
pater Europae 4
periodization 21
Persians (Aeschylus) 1–2
Petrarch 26–27
philology 15, 26–27
philosophi 23
philosophy 14–16, 24
Polo, Marco 11–13
Polti, Georges 33
The Prince (Machiavelli) 9–10
progress: and history 34; and time
27–29
Protestant Reformation 9, 15

Quintilian 22

Renaissance 27
republic of letters 16
Revolt of the Masses (Ortega y
Gasset) 31
Roman Church 8, 27
Roman Empire 3, 23, 32
romance epics 25–26
Rome (city) 25
Rome (republic and Empire) 3, 18

science, and philosophy 14–15
scientific advancement 28
scientific method 15

Scythians 5
Second World War 17
Shadow of Tomorrow (Huizinga) 31
silver 14
Spain, and the Americas 13–14
Spengler, Oswald, *The Decline of
the West* 30
Spinoza, Baruch 15
stemma codicum 15

technological superiority 14
techological advancement 28
textual criticism 15
Thycidides 21
time: conceptions of 21, 26–27;
Medieval 24; and progress 27–29;
Spengler on 30
Tocqueville, Alexis de 32
tradition 22–24, 34–35
Treaty of Rome (1957) 18
Trubeckoj, N. 34

Ulysses 12, 19
Ulysses (Joyce) 18–19
United States 28, 32; *see also*
America
utopia 33–34

Valery, Paul 1
Valla, Lorenzo 27
Venetians 12–13
Vienna 18
Vingthuit siècles 'd' Europe (de
Rougemont) 21
Virgil, *Aeneid* 12
Voltaire 28; *Essais sur les Moeurs* 11
von Goethe, Johann Wolfgang 35
vortex 22

Western Christianity 6–7
Western Empire 4
Western Europe 7
Western Middle Ages 7
written documents 8–9; *see also*
European literature

Zibaldone (Leopardi) 22

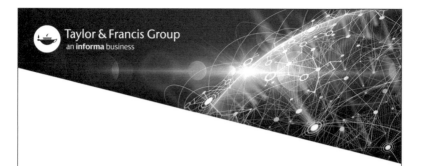